The Master Plan

Exit Strategy for Successful Business Owners

**Discover a Strategic Planning Formula for Maximum Company
Value, Strong Asset Protection and Work-Life Balance**

By

Peter G. Christman

Endorsements

"I have worked with Peter on programs for advisors and business owners and witnessed his commitment to the success of business owners while in business and after they exit their companies. This is a must read for business owners!"
Dr Donald F. Kuratko
The Jack M. Gill Distinguished Chair of EntrepreneurshipHey Carrie
Professor of Entrepreneurship; Executive & Academic Director;
Johnson Center for Entrepreneurship & Innovation
The Kelley School of Business

"We purchased one of our first companies from Peter in his early days as an investment banker and the transaction was a win-win for both buyer and seller. What sets Peter apart from other investment bankers is his holistic approach with clients that balances valuation with the client's need for a personal financial plan and a plan for living beyond the sale of the business."
Thomas S. Bagley | Pfingsten Partners, L.L.C.

"I have known and worked with Peter for over thirty years. He is the consummate professional who understands Business Owners and what they must do to plan for successfully selling and exiting their business."
Arthur Perrone, Vice-Chairman, The Geneva Companies

"Peter, as Co Founder of the Exit Planning Institute, has passionately written about a very important process for business owners no matter if they want to exit their company's now or in the future. It so important that business owners plan with their end game in mind! And do it the right way!!!"
John K. Paglia, Ph.D., CFA, CPA
Associate Dean; Associate Professor of Finance

4

The Master Plan

Pepperdine Grazizdio School of Finance

"I have known Peter and worked with him for over 30 years. That makes him old, not me. Peter has always demonstrated creative capabilities in dealing with business owners. We are both Founders of our mutual associations and have shared a lot of insightful conversations together. It is great to have Peter as a friend and a business alliance partner. Stay with Peter, he is sincere and competent in all his endeavors!! I know!!!!"
Michael R. Nall, CPA, CM&AA, CGMA
Founder, Alliance of Merger & Acquisition Advisors (AM&AA)
Co-Founder, MidMarket Alliance

"Peter Christman is the original exit coach –this book is a must read for business owners and their advisers looking to understand how to maximise the value of their business and achieve a successful exit. Peter's practical approach is based on his many years hands on experience in guiding owners thru this important process."
Craig West
CEO | B.Bus (Mgmt), M.Bus (Acct/Fin), M.Tax Law, CPA, CEPA

"I have known Peter for a long time and we definitely share a lot of the same beliefs for business owners and family businesses. It is a pleasure to work with him on various projects in which to educate these owners."
Dr. James Weiner
Principal | Author of The Legacy Conversation

"There are very few people in business today that I trust implicitly. Peter Christman is one of those people. A great thinker, a thought leader, and a person that I greatly admire. His pioneering thinking on Exit & Succession planning, personal and strategic planning has shown others a path through a myriad of confusion. Well done Peter on the new book. This takes off where the last book left off. A powerful sequel in the series."
Peter Hickey|CEO
MAUS Business Systems

"Pete Christman knows this simple truth: if you own your

business, eventually you won't.   Most people are so preoccupied with running their company that they fail to thoughtfully plan for the future. Want to leave your business on your terms? Make sure you read "The Master Plan".
Larry Gard, Ph.D.
President | Hamilton-Chase Consulting

"Peter Christman understands better than anyone that business owners facing a transition have a lot on their mind. So it's no surprise that he has once again broken new ground into the needs of business owners to have a "Master Plan" that goes much deeper than most of the other strategic processes that exist today. Without a clear plan in all of the three areas Peter's book outlines, many business owners will lack the motivation to pull the trigger on their planning and most will not have a fulfilling new life after their business sale or transfer. The risks for owners, families and employees are much too high to not give this book a careful read."
Bill Black, Founder and Host,
The Exit Coach Radio Network

"Peter Christman is one of the true visionaries in the field of middle market business owner transition planning. He is a co-founder of the Exit Planning Institute (EPI), the standard in the industry for professionals helping clients during this challenging phase in their career. Peter brings to the table the invaluable experience and insights of assisting hundreds of business owners and leading the nationally recognized faculty from the EPI."
Scott D. Miller, CPA/ABV
President Enterprise Services, Inc.
Author of "Buyouts" and "Navigating Mergers and Acquisitions"

"The author's analysis, coming from decades of experience, is "spot on". Business owners have been deeply educated on how to minimize income taxes, build personal wealth, and protect their assets from the claims of creditors but few if any have been properly exposed to the very important fundamentals examined in the book. Business value drivers

6

The Master Plan

are rarely examined prior to a transition and business owners are often surprised as to the result. Planning for a successful and rewarding exit requires an in-depth look at both financial and non-financial issues and the author brings a wealth of experience and insight into that process."
Sam G. Torolopoulos, CPA/ABV, ASA

"Peter, one of his clients and I have served on ABA panels together. I have witnessed first hand the impressive results and gratification Peter has obtained for his clients. He is truly committed to the success of the process for the client regardless of what may be in it for him financially. It's a quality often lacking in professionals. Don't miss out on his wisdom."
Jared Kaplan
Senior Counsel | McDermott Will & Emery

Dedication

There are many people to whom I would like to dedicate this book, but there are too many wonderful individuals who have influenced my work and life to mention here.

But there are a few that can't go unmentioned...

My terrific, fabulous and biggest supporter, my soul mate, my partner, and my wife......................Joyce Day!! She has had a tremendous, loving and positive effect on my life, for which I will be forever grateful.

My two wonderful sons, Rafe and Grant, who I raised from the fourth and sixth grades, respectively, and still love so much today.

Chris Snider, who is taking the banner of the Exit Planning Institute and is doing a terrific job of moving my international vision forward with tremendous energy and passion.

My writing coach, who has carried me longer than my mother, on this project.

My clients, who have created and developed a life time of wonderful experiences for me that resulted in friendships that will never go away because of the personal issues we worked on together.

Finally, to all the hard working, committed, focused business owners who want to be a success in their personal and business lives: I hope they wake up and realize they don't have to try doing it all on their own. They need a team to build the Master Plan on the legs of the three-legged stool to achieve success and life's fulfillment!

Table of Contents

Foreword by Christopher Snider
February 8, 2015

I'm sitting in my hotel room thinking about the Alliance of Mergers and Acquisitions Advisors (AMAA) thought leader of the year awards. I'm a finalist this year as a result of the Value Acceleration Methodology we have created and are teaching around the world. The methodology is a roadmap for how to implement exit strategy for business owners. I'm thinking about who I want to thank if I'm fortunate enough to win. Success at this level is never accomplished alone. There are always people that have steered you towards success; people who have planted ideas; people who have encouraged you along the way; people you trust and respect. I don't have to think long. Two names immediately pop into my head. My son of course is one. The other is Peter Christman.

I first met Pete in Chicago at the Exit Planning Institute's (EPI) Certified Exit Planning Advisor (CEPA) program in the fall of 2008. People who know Pete know he fills the room with wisdom and humor. At the time I didn't realize how lucky I would be to meet him and how he would come to change my life professionally and personally.

It's now 2011 and my partner and I have fully embraced the teachings of EPI, a company Pete cofounded in 2006. My partner and I are struggling to figure out how to launch our exit planning practice. I decide to call Pete to ask for his advice. He offers to meet with us if we make the trip to Chicago. My partner and I are so impressed with Peter's ideas we make several more monthly treks to Chicago to meet with Pete. Pete helps us launch the first local chapter. Then he helps us organize the first national EPI conference.

Today, in addition to a thriving exit planning private practice, which we are about to take worldwide, I am the owner and CEO of EPI. We now have 350 advisors in seven countries and nine local chapters in New York City, Cleveland, Chicago, Dallas, San Francisco, Southern California, Southern Nevada, St. Louis, and Sydney Australia and we are leading a transformation in the industry that will change transition outcomes for business owners and their families. There are others besides Pete that have helped us arrive here. But most of what we teach today is the result of not only those first few meetings with Pete but all his ideas and leadership since.

Peter Christman is a man ahead of his time. He is an icon in the industry. In exit planning circles Pete is affectionately regarded as "The Original". I tell students that attend our CEPA program today that if they really want to build a practice focused on helping owners and their families prosper through a transition they need to make one call - to Peter Christman. Then they simply need to do what he suggests you do.

Peter was on the forefront of the exit planning movement since the turn of the millennium. It started with a simple question, "Are we meeting our client's objectives?" It sounds like a pretty basic question. But it is amazing how many advisors don't ask. Yes Pete was doing some amazing things for his clients as an investment banker back in the 90's and early 2000's. But that was not enough for Pete. Pete knew there was more to it than just making money for his clients. He knew that for an owner to be fully successful with their transition we need to do more than just help them achieve their business objectives. We also need to make sure the owners personal and financial objectives are aligned with their business objectives.

Pete's analogy is the three legs of a stool. The first leg is maximizing value. The second, making sure the owner has planned financially from an estate and tax standpoint. And third, making sure the owner has planned for their third act. If any of these are missing the stool won't stand. And if one leg comes up short the stool is wobbly at best. To really achieve a successful transition all three legs must be aligned.

EPI in partnership with Grant Thornton, PNC Bank, and the Ohio Employee Ownership Center of Kent State University conducted a survey of business owners in 2013. The survey revealed:

83% of owners have no written transition plan; 49% have done no planning at all.

93% do not have a formal life after plan.

40% have no plans in place to cover illness, death or forced exit.

50% feel ownership transition plans require the company to remain profitable for plans to be properly executed; yet 86% have not taken on a strategic review or a value enhancement project.

56% felt they had a good idea of what their business is worth yet only 18% have had a formal valuation in the last two years.

A tidal wave of ownership transitions is surely coming as the baby boomer generation ages. Based on the data of our survey, EPI estimates that potentially 4.5 million businesses may transition in the next 10 years representing over $10 trillion of wealth transfer; the largest wealth transfer in history. Only the best prepared will be successful.

The stakes are both economically and socially enormous. 63% of the privately held businesses are owned by baby boomers and 80-90% of their net worth is tied up in their businesses. Yet most owners are not taking action to prepare for what is surely the most significant financial event of their lives. Although many owners don't want to admit it's likely to be at the top of their most significant emotional and psychological event of their lives as well.

Now with Master Planning Pete has taken his philosophy and turned it into a management and life planning system that not only helps owners achieve a successful transition but he shows owners that these are needed to achieve best in class performance in life. Those of us that are business owners know that business is more than just about the money; it's personal. By fully aligning all three legs owners can fully realize their dreams of not only succeeding in business but passing a legacy, protecting and maximizing family values and wealth, and achieving a fulfilled life in their third act.

There is another piece of advice Pete gave me. He says there are a lot of people that CAN do but not a lot of people that WILL do. My advice to you who have acquired this book is to keep it on your desk and refer to it frequently. Use it as your guide. You will achieve things you never thought possible, professionally AND personally. My advice is simple. Just do what Peter Christman is suggesting in this book. It's really quite that simple. At least it has been for those of us that have accepted his advice.

Christopher Snider, CEPA
CEO Exit Planning Institute
CEO Succession Plus USA

A Letter from the Author

Dear Business Owner,

Everyone is going to exit his or her business... it's just a matter of how and when!

When I thought about writing The Master Plan, I didn't envision a hefty, technical tone or tome. I think that sends the wrong message (that planning your business legacy is too hard, too time-consuming and too technical for the average business owner to undertake while they have other pressing responsibilities). It isn't. This is a concise guide designed primarily so YOU, the busy business owner, can see the value and begin moving towards being a Master Business Owner.

A Master Plan is a living document (in that you might add or revise elements of your Master Plan over time). It allows the reader to recognize the current value of their business, external forces that could negatively impact the company in case of a transfer of ownership (for example, taxes). The Master Plan also provides a clear plan for how to transfer those assets when the time comes. You can think of it the same way you would think of writing a will to protect your personal assets and to leave instructions for the care of your family and company.

The reason that you need to consider the creation of a Master Plan is because, unlike a will, the Master Plan isn't only critical in the wake of an owner's death. It provides a plan for

15

the 5 Ds of business exits: Death, Disability, Divorce, Distress, Disagreement. We'll talk more about the 5 Ds of business exits more in a later chapter.

The 5 Ds can happen to anyone at any age. My advice is to follow the guideline: if you're human, if you a have a heartbeat and if you own a business... well, then you need to start Master Planning.

Perhaps you aren't ready to think about exiting your business. In fact, you might not want to sell or exit at all. So why do a Master Plan? First, it's just a good business practice, but it also functions as an insurance policy for the continuity of the business. It serves as a contingency plan in case anything happens to the business owner.

You know, every so often business owners receive unsolicited offers from buyers for which they are unprepared. Once they decide to proceed with only one buyer, they risk proceeding without a Master Plan to protect them from leaving too much money on the table, paying too much to Uncle Sam and having seller's remorse.

With a Master Plan in place, you are always prepared and ready for those unsolicited offers and situations. And, of course, having a Master Plan means having higher cash flows and greater business value.

There are great professionals out there that can work with you to develop a great Master Plan. It's crucial that all business owners have a Master Plan. It's equally important for those owners to have a good understanding of what a Master Plan is so that they can thoroughly review and understand what professionals will provide.

Master Planning is an integrative process. Accountants, CPAs, Attorneys and other advisors/consultants are not trained or certified in this area. Unfortunately, that's because the motivation just isn't there for them to work together in order to work for you. These professionals aren't compensated based on their ability to create additional value for your company or to save you money.

That's the reason I wrote this book. I want to walk you through the process of creating a Master Plan so that you will understand the terminology, the process, and the expected results as you develop your own Master Plan.

I've broken down the entire process into four stages, which I describe in a following chapter. I'll also share with you some great case studies that illustrate the most important parts of each phase. At the end of this book, I'll provide you with a way you can reach out to me if you're ready to commit to creating your own Master Plan.

Peter G. Christman
Founder Master Planning Institute
CoFounder Exit Planning Institute
Founder The Christman Group

*I have been sharing the poem, "What Will Matter"
by Michael Josephson, for years since it was
given to me by Mikki Williams, Vistage Group
Leader, International Speaker and friend. Each
time I share it with my clients and at speaking
engagements it allows them to absorb this very
important process with an open heart. Now, I'd
like to share it with you.*

WHAT WILL MATTER
by Michael Josephson

Ready or not, some day it will all come to an
end.
There will be no more sunrises, no minutes,
hours, or days.
All the things you collected, whether treasured
or forgotten, will pass to someone else.
Your wealth, fame, and temporal power will
shrivel to irrelevance.
It will not matter what you owned or what you
were owed.
Your grudges, resentments, frustrations, and
jealousies will finally disappear.
So, too, your hopes, ambitions, plans, and to-do
lists will expire.
The wins and losses that once seemed so important
will fade away.
It won't matter where you came from or what side
of the tracks you lived on at the end.
It won't matter whether you were beautiful or

18

The Master Plan

brilliant.
Even your gender and skin color will be
irrelevant.
So what will matter? How will the value of your
days be measured?
What will matter is not what you bought but what
you built; not what you got but what you gave.
What will matter is not your success but your
significance.
What will matter is not what you learned but what
you taught.
What will matter is every act of integrity,
compassion, courage,
or sacrifice that enriched, empowered, or
encouraged others to emulate your example.
What will matter is not your competence but your
character.
What will matter is not how many people you knew
but how many will feel a lasting loss when you're
gone.
What will matter is not your memories but the
memories that live in those who loved you.
What will matter is how long you will be
remembered, by whom, and for what.
Living a life that matters doesn't happen by
accident.
It's not a matter of circumstance but of choice.
Choose to live a life that matters.

CHAPTER ONE

Prepare for Life's Certainties

> "In this world nothing can be said to be certain, except death and taxes."
> Benjamin Franklin

What does the 23-year old Silicon Valley start-up founder have in common with the 52-year old owner of a million-dollar family business and the CEO of a major conglomerate? They each need an exit strategy.

There are two kinds of business owners in the world - the first is the typical business owner. This type of business owner is so busy working in their business that they don't have to work on their business. Putting out fires monopolizes their time, and they have not mastered the skills necessary to move towards building their business.

21

The second kind of business owner is the Master Business Owner. The Master Business Owner (or MBO) has a master business plan that prepares them and their business for the future. The MBO has successfully mastered the skills of running their business and now they are successfully mastering the building of their business. The MBO has a complete exit strategy planned for their business. The Master Business Owner has a Master Plan Exit Strategy.

To illustrate the importance of being an MBO and having a Master Plan Exit Strategy, let's take a look at the following statistics:

- 50% of Business Owners want to exit their business within the next 5 years and 75% want to exit within the next 10 years;
- 80% of All Business Owners have 90% of their net worth tied up in their business;
- 83% of business owners have no written Master Plan.*

Any financial planner or wealth manager will tell you that this doesn't make for a good investment strategy. Perhaps more telling is that 50% of businesses do not survive the death of their owner. For many businesses (50%, in fact!), all of the effort, resources, and time invested into the business has suddenly disappeared. If you think about the negative impact that leaving your business without an exit plan can have on your family, your employees, your vendors and your customers, you get sick to your stomach - then you're beginning to understand the importance of having a Master Plan.

50% of business owners exit their businesses through the 5 Ds: Death, Disability, Divorce, Distress, and Disagreement. Thankfully, the 5 Ds are not unforeseeable (as 50% of exited business owners will tell you) - they aren't Acts of God that no one could have possibly expected. A Master Business Owner not only expects the 5 Ds, but they take strategic steps towards mitigating the potential impact of the 5 Ds by preparing a clear, well thought out Master Plan.

Master Planning is a conscious effort to maximize enterprise value while enabling the conversion of that ownership into personal financial freedom and peace of mind. The Master Plan takes all the legal issues, business issues, value creation issues, financial issues and personal issues and addresses all of them in the Master Plan. Master Planning consists of strategic planning, exit planning, profit improvement planning, financial strategy, personal financial strategies, estate planning, tax planning and life transition planning.

Your best bet is to stay ahead of the 5 Ds!

Remember - you will exit your business sooner or later (one way or another!) This can be an overwhelming concept but it doesn't have to be! By the time you read this book and review the valuable resources, you'll have a much better understanding of how to maximize the value of your organization. Be sure you have complete asset protection and maybe most importantly a clearer vision of what life looks like for you once you continue on to the next phase of your life.

For valuable resources from this book that will take the overwhelm and/or anxiety out of starting the process in laying a firm foundation which will promote a smooth exit strategy, visit
www.MasterPlanningInstitute.com or text MPI to 58885

CHAPTER TWO

How to Use This Book to Change Your Financial
Life

"Time is more valuable than money. You can get more money,
but you cannot get more time."
Jim Rohn

I spent 17 years in corporate management with two fine
companies: Ford Motor Company and Xerox Corporation. And
then I came to a point in time in my life where I wanted to get
into my own business and become an entrepreneur and I
looked around at many opportunities, couldn't find one that
was available that met my criteria, and I got into investment
banking. Selling companies that would have values between
five and a hundred and fifty million that were all privately

owned.

In 1985, I started the Chicago office for the world's largest valuator of businesses and seller of middle market companies in the five to a 150 million ranges. 1992, I left this company and hung out my shingle and started a boutique firm in Chicago, Illinois with seven other investment bankers on my team. We successfully sold our clients' companies for the highest value/ best value possible because of our proprietary auction process, but it turned out that we could have gotten even better value. With decent Master Planning, our clients could have kept much more of what they got.

We realized that our clients were losing monetary value after their sale because they were paying too much in taxes. There was no tax planning. As an investment banker, I wasn't sure the money was going where it should be going because there was no estate planning.

All the planning was taking place (and often still does, unfortunately) after the liquidity event instead of before the liquidity event. By reversing the process and leading with strategy, our clients received and kept the greatest value for all of their efforts and accomplishments through the use of a Master Plan Exit Strategy.

That's how and why I got started in exit planning and Master Planning.

I had a client that was selling a company, and their attorney was in a different state. About three weeks prior to the closing and sale of the business, the owner calls me and says, "I don't want everyone to know I'm getting all this money, Can you help me out?"

My jaw dropped. Less than a month before closing and no planning had taken place - that left my client susceptible even

The Master Plan

as I marched him into the wealth management division at a bank in Chicago. They couldn't roll out the red carpet fast enough for a man about to receive over forty million in cash and without a plan for how he was going to use it.

And trust me, if you don't have a plan for your money you can trust that someone else does. Will that plan align with your goals, your lifestyle and your wishes? Who knows?

It's instances like that that gave me the wake-up call in the summer of 2000. In 2005, after co-writing the "10 Trillion Opportunity" I co-founded the Exit Planning Institute to train and certify advisors in the process of exit planning. And since that time, our firm has trained and certified advisors from seven different countries, to work with clients to have their Master Plan align with their plan and not the plans of a well-meaning advisor or not-so-well meaning advisor.

I sold the Exit Planning Institute in 2012 to a consulting group headed by Chris Snider who is doing a great job of leading the Institute nationally and internationally (www.exit-planning-institute.org).

I'm still active on the board of directors of the Exit Planning Institute. I still teach at their certification classes and travel around the world to speak about exit planning. But, I was trying to find the next step to get business owners off the dime, to start working on exit planning.

This book is written especially for privately held business owners whose businesses range from 1 million dollars in revenues to 200 million dollars in revenues.

Their age can be anywhere from in their 20s to owners in their 80s, whether male or female. Whether the owner has a manufacturing business, distribution business or service business. If you are human and you have a heartbeat, you qualify for starting the Master Planning process.

This book will change how you manage your company for creating value versus lifestyle management. It will show you how to maximize the value of your business when it comes time to transfer it. You will learn how to keep most of the value when you liquefy your business. Finally, you will receive the benefits of going through a life planning assessment and establishing new goals, objectives, and life balance. At a basic level, this book will help you shift your mindset to value creation instead of lifestyle creation, therefore yielding higher value enterprise companies, greater cash flow, greater financial benefits. And then how to keep those benefits.

The good news is people have taken action, and the results have been staggering. John, a rural business owner, running a family business that he and his wife, Mary, worked in for over 15 years, was able to plan his exit around a 35 million cash exit by developing his own Master Plan and building what I call his three-legged stool.

Every time I would enter my client's building, Mary would shoot me a look that could scare buzzards. John finally confided in me that Mary had always thought the business would go to their only son, a young man in the first years of high school, and she thought the time and resources necessary to create a Master Plan was a waste of time. She wasn't worried about the potential risk – she was happy to wait for their son to mature and qualify his interest in the business. John wanted to do something while the firm was at its pinnacle of success.

Today, Mary has nothing but smiles for me. Because of John and Mary's Master Plan, the couple was able to leverage the value of their business to create the financial freedom they are now enjoying, according to their plan. So, in Mary's mind, I am

28

the greatest thing since sliced bread.

You can benefit too! Business owners who have developed and implemented Master Plans have realized the satisfaction of achieving their lifetime goals of maximum company value, personal financial planning success and a new life of enjoyment and fulfillment.

This book will change how you manage your company for creating value versus for lifestyle. It will demonstrate how to maximize the value of your company when it comes time to transfer it. You will learn how to keep most of the value when you liquefy your business, and finally you will receive the benefits of going through a life planning assessment and establishing new personal goals and objectives.

In the next section, we'll introduce you to the three-legged stool system that we use to break down the Master Planning process into easier, shorter chunks. Then, I'll share other compelling case studies with you - so you can see the three-legged stool system in action.

For valuable resources from this book that will take the overwhelm and/or anxiety out of starting the process in laying a firm foundation which will promote a smooth exit strategy, visit
www.MasterPlanningInstitute.com or text MPI to 58885

> "The first step toward success is taken when you refuse to be a captive of the environment in which you first find yourself."
> Mark Caine

The Story of John, Mary and the 35 Million Dollar Exit

I've already introduced you to John and Mary, the couple that owned a family business for over fifteen years, who planned a thirty-plus million-dollar exit through his development of his own Master Plan.

Because of his great success with using a Master Plan, I asked him if he'd allow me to share his story with you so that you could learn from the strategies that he used.

John's company was positioned to take advantage of the lack of innovation in his industry. John made sure that his company was creating innovative solutions to solve his customers' problems. Having the right product, John focused his attentions on selling those products to the right clients.

John spent the majority of his time on the road, building his business to over 70 employees and 25 million dollars a year in sales. But when it became clear that his teenaged son wasn't interested in following dad's footsteps and entering the family business, John and his wife Mary had to take a hard look at the future that they imagined for themselves.

Fifteen years building a family business is plenty of time for the company to become riddled with accounting, management and succession issues. But John and I spent three years working

The Master Plan

on his Master Plan so that John felt comfortable making the decision about what would happen when (not if) he exited his company.

At first, it was obvious that Mary wasn't a big fan of John's work and investment in a Master Plan. John and Mary's only son was still young and they – as a couple – had always believed the business would naturally just pass on to their son. That was the plan, so why – Mary wondered – did they need a Master Plan that would take years to create and involve inviting advisors into their lives and business?

But John understood his son's disinterest in the business and didn't want to rely on the possibility of his son taking over the business one day. The company was at the pinnacle of its success, but John was spending more time on the road than he was at home with his family. After fifteen years, John wondered if there was a better way.

John and I developed his Master Plan. He ran an extremely clean business, and he is, what I refer to as, a Master Business Owner. He didn't run a business to line his pockets; the business was never his private piggy bank like many 'lifestyle business owners.' There were no problems in the business – no financial issues, no environmental issues, no personnel issues. The biggest issue that John would have to overcome was that John was so involved in the day-to-day tasks that made the company so profitable.

Because John's continued involvement, if only to transition the business to the new owners, was so important – something we learned during our analysis for his Master Plan – it was crucial that we were very specific about John and Mary's plans for the future so that we could negotiate the terms of John sticking around after the transfer of the business.

31

"We were doing business all over the world. The company was doing well, but I was traveling all the time. I knew that I either needed to bring on additional employees or I needed to look for a new owner," John told me. "To protect my family and our assets, we chose that time to liquidate what I had in the business and sell it."

John's 'offer' clearly stated what he'd do for the first six months after the transfer and then he was going to withdraw from his involvement in the business.

"I would have had to bring people in from the outside. They probably wouldn't have had the same views that I did of how to run our family organization," John said. "I would be risking what I had built. Instead, if I sold it then I would receive a great value for the efforts I had put into the business and the new owner would have all the risk and liability of building the company further."

Because John had such a clear idea of how he wanted the sale and the transition of his company to go, it took about a year and a half to find the right buyer. He not only got everything he expected, he got more. To the tune of 35 million dollars cash!

Mary is pretty happy with me. While John and Mary gave up the opportunity to leave the business to their only son, the sale of their business ended up strengthening their net worth (approximately 75-80% of their net worth was tied up in the business. Not a very healthy financial position). They were able to take the profits from the sale and diversify their investments. Now, they weren't only one emergency away from personal financial disaster.

They were also able to realize their personal vision of their future earlier than they would have been able to otherwise, had they continued in the business. They were able to leave their

32

The Master Plan

business at the pinnacle of its value and walk away with an excellent return on their investment.

When I asked if John had any advice to share with other business owners, he said he wanted to add this, "None of us is invincible, and you need a backup plan. As a business owner, we have two priorities: our family and our business. Business owners need to realize that they need a backup plan to protect both of these things."

CHAPTER THREE

The First Step

Great! You've taken the first step. You've turned the page and are showing interest that will impact you and your family exponentially.

The first step of the Master Plan is to develop your team. You might be thinking, "Team? Why do I need a team?" A Master Plan team consists of a team representing many different skills and backgrounds, but the 'heartbeat' of the teams is what we refer to as the Quarterback. The Quarterback coordinates the efforts of the entire team and makes sure that their work aligns with your goals.

During the first phase, Leg One, you will need to have Value Enhancement Advisors on your team. During Leg Two, of the stool, you'll need to add your financial, estate and tax advisors. During Leg Three, you will again rely on your Master Plan coordinator and if needed, life planning psychologists. Other Advisors will be called in to consult as part of the team process.

When I work with my client on a Master Plan, my role is that of the quarterback.

The Master Plan Coordinator or the quarterback of the team

should be someone trained in Master Planning and exit planning. I would recommend contacting the Exit Planning Institute out of Cleveland, Ohio to find out who is a Certified Exit Planning Advisor in your area.

This person will also assist in developing other members of the team, for instance, the value enhancement advisors will be different from company to company.

After performing the original assessment during Leg One, it may be determined that you need sales and marketing assistance or that you require additional advisors. Your quarterback will know who the experts are in your particular locale, and they will make recommendations on whom to bring in as part of the action plan.

Each leg of the stool begins with a thorough analysis and assessment of that section. Leg one begins with a market valuation of your business. There are a lot of ways to value a business, but the starting point here is a "market" valuation. That means what a willing buyer would pay a willing seller.

There are a lot of different ways to value a business covered in technical books on the subject. But if you have a competent Master Planning Advisor assisting you, they will know how to perform the initial valuation and explain it to you.

Notice I said "initial." It is only the beginning point, and you don't need an expensive valuation to begin the process. Valuating a business is an art, not a science.

A firm or advisor, which is very familiar with the "market" value or what your company would sell for today, should perform the valuation! That is the starting point of Leg One.

Next your advisor will ask you a lot of questions about your business operations, industry, management, employees, customers, sales, and marketing, etc. The answers to these questions will determine how you stand on the factors that most buyers are interested in and whether these factors add value or subtract value.

It is this analysis of your buyer attractiveness and readiness factors that will determine your future course of action. It will boil down to the decision of "whether you transfer your business now or develop an action plan of corrective steps to improve your buyer value factors."

This Master Planning analysis of leg one will factor in how long actions would take to implement and how much investment would be needed to accomplish these actions.

In a lot of cases, these steps are particularly necessary for changing from a "lifestyle" management technique to a "value creation" management technique.

No one should be operating a business without knowing the factors that are adding business value and the factors that are deterring business value! Sounds obvious, but unfortunately it's just not common practice.

In the following two legs of the stool, the business owner will start building relationships with financial wealth managers, estate planning personnel, and tax advisors. If you, as the business owner, are not familiar with the experts in these areas, your quarterback will have knowledge of the professionals who can assist in helping with Leg Two of the process.

The third leg of the stool is the most neglected leg in the stool. Why? There are many reasons for this. The business owner is so immersed in their business that they don't plan for anything else in their personal lives.

Facing one's mortality is another common issue we see. Taking the time to think through the "why" of where you have been and the "where" of where you are headed may not seem like a priority right now. Many business owners make major business decisions based on circumstance and without any forethought.

I understand that it takes a lot to look in the mirror and ask yourself tough questions, because usually you don't like the answers. But those who don't build this portion of the stool often fall victim to one of the "5 D's" discussed earlier in the book. For as neglected as this piece of the process is, business owners don't realize how it drives the whole future of a business owner.

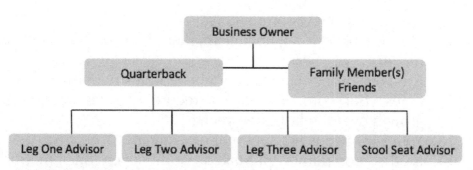

When I speak in front of business owners on the subject of Master Planning and exit planning around the country (and around the globe), I like to start with a quiz of twenty questions. I usually read these questions aloud and ask the audience to assign 5 points to every question to which they answer "Yes." You can play along by reading the questions and noting the number of times you respond with Yes.

Twenty Questions

1. Have you had a formal written business evaluation completed within the last year?
2. Do you have a formal contingency plan in place in case you become incapacitated?
3. Do you have a strong management team in place?
4. Is your largest customer below 10% of your total company revenue?
5. Does the company have an active strategic business plan in place?
6. Are your products and services free of threats from global competition?
7. Is your equipment up to date and in good working order?
8. Is your industry growing?
9. Do you have few competitors?
10. Do you have a significant market share or a protective niche?
11. Are your profit margins at or above industry norms?
12. Does your company have a record of sales and profit growth over the last three years?
13. Your business is not seasonal or cyclical?
14. Is the company's pre-taxed profit over one million dollars?
15. Are your financial statements audited?
16. Do you have an updated personal, estate, tax and personal plan?
17. Do you have a current written succession, exit or transition plan?
18. Do you know exactly how much you will need to exit your business?
19. Do you know exactly what you would do with your life if

you exited the business?
20. Do you have a specific life personal plan in writing?

I am sure after reading these twenty questions you would agree that to be adequately prepared and to be assured of the maximum valuation of the company, the answers to these questions, all twenty, should be yes, (yes being the correct answer) A perfect score would be 100%. Each Yes is worth 5%.

I had given this quiz to approximately 2200 business owners*; here is how the results shook out:

- 35% received a score of less than 50%
- 35% received a score of 50%
- 30% received a score of 70% and below

Companies prepared to answer "Yes" more often to these questions often garner a greater value in the marketplace. If selling is their transfer method or exit, they will garner a higher value because of how prepared they have the business for that step.

My client, Roger, ran a business in the trucking industry. Roger was able to answer "Yes" to most of these questions. While trucking is not a glamorous industry, the average trucking company will sell for a multiple of three to four times **EBITDA**.

Terms You Should Know
EBITDA: Earnings before Interest, Taxes, Depreciation and Amortization
EBIT: Earnings before Interest and Taxes

Roger went through the Master Planning process and sold his company for a multiple of 7.3 times EBITDA, 5.3 times his net worth or company equity, 20.2 times a multiple of EBIT - and he did it during a recession. He was successful because he took the time to plan for the exit and transfer of his business. His investment banker approached 269 prospects. Twenty confidential business reviews were sent out after confidentiality agreements were received. Roger had three buyers visit his company; two made offers.

Stephen, another business owner, owned three companies that had cumulative revenues of over 50 million dollars. His exit was precipitated by one of the 5 Ds, and he was unprepared - there was no Master Plan, no value enhancement plan, no tax plan, no estate plan, and no financial plan. The only people that made any money off his exit were legal and accounting advisors and the government. His family was left with nothing!

As an advisor, it drives me crazy when I see how poor planning has led to divorce, families being pulled apart and in the most tragic circumstances, suicide. These were not stupid people; these were very qualified, brilliant people who simply failed to plan properly for the future.

The reason these situations occur so frequently is that in today's environment there is a plethora of business owners who run the business for the creation and maintenance of their lifestyle. They take out all the money they can in order to support their lifestyle. They run non-business expenses through the company accounts, and they pay minimal taxes because they concentrate their efforts on minimizing the taxable income and assets of the business.

Which sounds great, right? Who isn't interested in paying

fewer taxes? Who doesn't want to be able to afford the lifestyle of their dreams? All of that sounds great until it comes time to exit your business, and suddenly you are wondering why you cannot get more money for your company.

The value your business demonstrates is that of a minimally profitable company, or it appears unprofitable because of your write-offs against the business. You will be receiving multiples of one, two, or three at the most, four depending on the industry.

We call that a lifestyle management style.

Master Business Owners (MBOs) use what we call a value creation process of management. MBOs do not use their business to support their lifestyle, but they simply take out adequate compensation. As a result, when they go to transfer their business, they are demonstrating how well that business can do and they are getting multiples of 4 to 12 times the EBITDA depending on the industry!

Creating value leverages the business and the profits the business owner receives through that management style.

The issue between that lifestyle manager and value creation manager is that privately held businesses have a cost of capital that ranges between 20 – 30%. A privately held business owner will have to make or obtain returns that are greater than 20 – 30% just to create value and cover the risk of ownership. Statistics tell us that 80 – 90% of business owners are not meeting this standard and have no plans to do so. They are losing value every year in their business, and they are creating a **value gap**.

Terms You Should Know

Value Gap: the difference between what the market says the company is worth and what the business owner wants or thinks their business is worth.

What is the answer for privately held business owners? The answer is developing a Master Plan. The Master Plan, if you can visualize it, is like a three-legged stool. The seat of that stool is the master plan. Leg One consists of doing everything possible to maximize company value. To build Leg Two of the stool, the owner plans from an estate, tax and financial point of view so that they can keep most of the money they get when they transfer the business. The third leg of the stool is to create a life plan for life fulfillment and balance.

Why a three-legged stool? In order for a stool to be stable, it has to have three equally strong and equally sized legs on which to balance and distribute the weight of the seat. One weak leg will damage the overall strength of the stool. One shorter leg will ruin the balance.

We use the image of the stool to convey the importance of having a strong foundation in three areas that will help you balance and strengthen your plans for the future. That's the three-legged stool.

Let's delve into each piece of the three-legged stool and how they work together to make the Master Plan.

To find out more on how you can prepare your business to gain a top multiple at your liquidity event through Master Planning and value creation management,
visit
www.MasterPlanningInstitute.com
or text MPI to 58885

> "Creating Value is an inherently cooperative process, capturing value is inherently competitive."
> Barry J. Nalebuff

Jason Steps Away

As with John and Mary, Jason's business was family-owned, but it wasn't one he started. Jason's father was working at the company when the owner decided to sell. Jason's father gathered six partners to combine resources so they could purchase the business.

Jason started working at the company in the late 1960s during high school and then, after serving during the Vietnam war, Jason returned to the company full-time. After thirty years, Jason was the only remaining partner.

"I had been associated with this company since I was in high school. It was part of my life, a big part," Jason explains. "You kind of lose your identity after selling a business that was just a big part of your identity for so long."

Part of the Master Plan was to include a six-month transitional period for Jason so that he could acclimate to life without his company.

In the beginning, I met with Jason and his brother to make suggestions on how they could proceed in terms of positioning the company and their building for sale. Because the building they were using and going to sell had been around for so long, certain items had to be addressed before Jason would be able to

The Master Plan

sell the company.

"We were so focused on what our company was doing that day, that year, the next year that we couldn't distance ourselves enough to even think about selling it."

Once they had a plan, they had the objective and actionable steps that they would need to take in order to have a successful sale.

In the midst of this, Jason lost his brother and remaining partner in the business and decided it was time to remove himself from the company. I focused on preparing Jason, making sure he was fully educated in the options and helping him to focus on the long-term opportunities. Choices were now being made, in regards to debts and the building, which were positive in terms of selling the business – but would have otherwise been handled differently.

It wasn't easy for Jason to step away from his company, but he had a plan that he was able to stick with and now he spends his time traveling, playing golf and enjoying his time with friends.

"You kind of miss the challenges that drive you when you are running a business. But then again, you don't," Jason adds. "But it felt good to be able to leave the company knowing that my family there – the employees that had been part of my life for so long – had a smooth transition, too."

CHAPTER FOUR

Maximize Your Company Value

The primary goal of the first leg of the stool, Leg One, involves maximizing the value of the business to the fullest. Another primary goal of the First Leg of the stool is to restructure the organization's management style of the business, assuming you are not already operating under the Value Creation Process, rather than the typical Lifestyle Management process. Educating the business owner as to not only the differences between lifestyle and value creation but also the benefits they will derive from operating under the Value Creation Process is very important.

Leg One of the stool begins as each leg does, with an assessment of the business through a company valuation and operations reviews. This assessment analyzes and reviews, what is called in the industry, **buyer value factors**.

The Master Plan

Why is this important for sellers to understand? Buyers are NOT in love with your business! It's important to remember buyers might not value the same things in the business you do.

Because of this, we have developed what we call the 54 Buyer Value Factors that cover areas such as the personal factors, age, motivation of the owner, family partner consensus, whether the owner is realistic on value and so forth. The other areas that are analyzed are business operations, the industry that the company is in, sales and marketing programs and activities, legal and regulatory activities and economic factors affecting the company and the owners' plans.

From this analysis, an action plan is developed outlining the steps that will be needed to correct the deficiencies in the business operations. The action plan also includes a timetable for implementing these strategies along with the people who are going to be responsible for each step of the action plan.

The 54 Buyer Factors allow us to analyze the company as a buyer. A buyer who is looking for opportunities based on improvement and whether the change results has a positive or neutral impact on the business. These are factors that buyers consider and look at when they are determining the areas of strength and areas that need improvement for a particular company. What we do is we give the owner a report that says what the factor is, what it should be and how they rate on that factor based on the flagged opportunities for improvement.

When a client or potential client asks, "Why isn't my company worth more?" the answer could be anything from a faulty management team to customer concentration issues (instances where 90% of your business is to a single customer).

In total, we also use another 16 key Buyer Factors that mean you may be in trouble or conversely, that you are in good shape!

The 16 Key Indicators of Business Valuation Problems*:

BIG 6

- *Strength of Market Position*: If your company has strong market share or a protected niche in the industry, it will be more valuable.
- *Size* (it matters)
- *Revenue Growth* (Historical & Expected): The higher the revenues, the better. Company's revenues are in the upper half of all competitors in the industry or are of sufficient size that the Company could serve as a "platform" for consolidating a number of companies in the industry.
- *Revenue Concentration* (Customer, product, and channel)
- *Margins* (Gross and EBITDA): Higher gross margins are preferred but in any case the Company's gross margins are equal or better than industry norms.
- *Quality of Management Team*: Having a strong and experienced management team with demonstrated successes in place are valuable because it shows that the business (and its success) isn't dependent upon the owner.

10 Others Signs That Could Be Affecting Your Multiples:

48

The Master Plan

- *Breadth of Products and Services*
- *Quality of Products and Services*: Quality products (especially certified quality assessments) help differentiate your products and processes from the competitions'.
- *Seasonality*: sales, expenses, and capital do not vary significantly throughout the year.
- *Cyclicality*: Revenues are relatively unaffected by economic cycles.
- *Working Capital Investment Needed*
- *Quality of Infrastructure* (systems and facilities)
- *Level of Capital Expenditures*
- *Potential Contingent Liabilities*
- *Quality of Management Processes*
- *Financial Process and Controls*

We begin Leg One with a market valuation of your business. There are a lot of ways to value a business, but the starting point here is a 'market' valuation. That means what a willing buyer would pay a willing seller.

There are a lot of different ways to value a business that are covered in a lot of technical books on the subject. A competent Master Planning advisor will know how to perform the initial valuation and explain it to you.

Notice I said "initial." This first valuation is only the beginning point, and you don't need an expensive assessment to begin the process. Assessing a business' value is an art, not a science.

A firm or advisor, which is very familiar with "market" value or what your company would sell for today, as it sits now, should perform the valuation! That is the starting point of Leg One.

Next, your advisor will ask you a lot of questions about your business operations, industry, management, employees, customers, sales, and marketing, etc. The answers to these questions will determine how you stand on the factors that most buyers are interested in and whether these factors add   or subtract value from your organization.

It is this analysis of your buyer attractiveness and readiness factors that will determine your future course of action. It will boil down to the decision of 'whether you transfer your business now or develop an action plan of corrective steps to improve your buyer value factors.'

This master planning analysis during Leg One will factor into how long actions would take to implement and how much investment would be needed to accomplish these changes. In a lot of cases these steps are particularly necessary for changing from a "lifestyle" management technique to a "value creation" management technique.

Take Note!

No one should be operating a business without knowing the factors that are adding business value and the factors that are deterring business value! Sounds obvious, but in reality, it is not common practice!

So as I mentioned earlier, after this analysis, the results of this analysis are an action plan to remedy the deficiencies that this analysis brings up in the operations. This process could take as long as 12 - 24 months. It may necessitate the owner making additional investments in the business; discussions will be held with the owner's quarterback and advisor as to the pros and cons of these action plans and investment.

All of this work is dependent upon the nature of each business in conjunction with the owner's goals and objectives.

In a later chapter, we'll review exactly how those goals and objectives can have a major impact on the Master Plan.

Now that you have a better understanding of why its important to review your organization from a buyers perspective, you can download the complete Value Factor Ratings by visiting:
www.MasterPlanningInstitute.com or text MPI to 58885

> "A good financial plan is a road map that shows us exactly
> how the choices we make today will affect our future"
> Alexa Von Tobel

Brian's Plan for (No) Succession

Brian had three sons, two of whom were working in the business with him when he approached his family over Thanksgiving with a single question:
What did they want to do?

Brian's business was in the chemical industry and while they were able to pivot their business out of highs and lows by changing the product and sub-industries they were selling into, Brian wasn't sure what the next steps should be.

There was a lot of pressure on the family members to make the right decision. Brian's father (the boys' grandfather) had started the company, and that was a big part of their decision. Brian had decided that no matter what, he wanted to have the entire family buy-in to the final decision, or he wouldn't do it.

During Master Planning we talk about the importance of having buy-in from your family (if you're in a family run business), but a third-generation business could have it's own mega-truck full of family drama attached to it. So it was extremely smart of Brian to insist that everyone agree.

His son that wasn't involved in the operations of the business told his father that he was happy with whatever decision the group made, and the two sons that were working alongside their dad were hesitant but hopeful when they said they were interested in selling, under the right circumstances and could they test the waters.

"I knew that if I were to stay in the business that it would take a large financial commitment on my part. At sixty, I wasn't sure I wanted to take on that level of debt," Brian describes. "So over Thanksgiving, we sat around the table outside. I had a notebook with three or four different options that I thought were viable, and the boys wanted to spend some time looking into the option of selling the business."

Brian's first step was to get the business ready to sell. This requires a lot of time and effort, but by putting himself in the shoes of his ideal buyer, Brian was able to knock out a list of changes.

"I got everything in line. Accounting, payables, receivables, we had everything ready to go so that if anyone walked in the door and asked about the business, we could tell them and we would be able to look them in the eye knowing it was 100% the truth."

When Brian and I discussed the maximum value that he could get for his business, I urged him to stay on for a certain amount of time. I suggested six months, maybe a year, but Brian decided to stay on a little longer than that (like, ten years longer!). Brian counts himself extremely lucky to remain an important part of the business, even while he no longer has to shoulder the responsibilities, liabilities and risk of growing a business.

"A lot of guys sell their businesses, and the first thing they do is get a Corvette then they get a girlfriend," Brian jokes. "It's because they didn't have a plan. 75% of all business owners that sell regret it later, but that's because they did not plan for how their life would be post-sale."

CHAPTER FIVE

Personal Financial Planning and Asset Protection

In the previous story, I talked about how Brian had to put himself in the shoes of his ideal buyer and take a long look at the business he wanted to sell. In order to get top dollar, you have to be able to claim that your business is doing well and have the proof to back up your claims. This might require months or even years of "cleaning the skeletons out of the closet" before you even put your business up for sale.

In completing a developed action plan you are maximizing the value of your business in your buyer's eyes, the next step in the process of working with our team is having a clear understanding of Asset Protection, what we affectionately refer to as Leg Two. This is where we start working on personal, financial, estate and tax planning.

We want to have a financial plan that helps us to achieve goals and objectives that we are going to set up during Leg Two. We want to make sure that we know what are "needs" versus "wants" and what we can have. We want to have a process that will minimize the taxes on a business transfer or exit. We want to make sure that, at the time of that exit, we have done everything possible to keep most of what we are getting.

Next, we'll discuss legacy issues through estate planning efforts. We would use your advisors for this process, but if you or your other advisors are not comfortable with your advisors (or your quarterback is not comfortable with your advisors), this is the time to spark a discussion with your quarterback.

Because the average advisor isn't experienced in the process that we are recommending, it may take some time to acclimate your advisors to not work in silos. The 3 Legged Stool process breaks down those silos and integrates the expertise of each silo in the team-type of environment. So your quarterback will assist you if you do not feel you have adequate representation in the three areas of wealth management, estate planning, and tax planning.

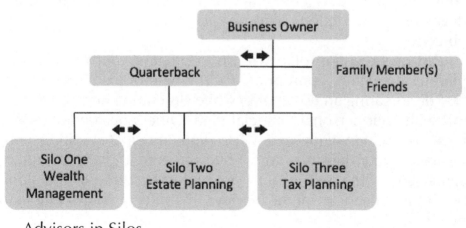

Advisors in Silos

Take Note!
Silos are insular systems. That means they are, by definition, incapable of reciprocal relationships. When we talk about advisors being "silos," we are talking about advisors that are incapable (due to past experience or lack of skills) of integrating their work with that of other advisors. The Master Plan system integrates advisors into a team that works on behalf of the business owner.

There are a lot of considerations in working through each stage of the assessment process. The first step will be sitting down with advisors to find out where you are currently at, what your financial goals and objectives are, and working toward developing an action plan to accomplish your goals and objectives.

Part of the action plan will be to prepare your personal tax plan in a structure appropriate for the type of Exit. The same is true of preparing an estate plan while structuring and combining this with your personal financial plan. Other considerations you have to include your age when you anticipate exiting your business, your lifestyle, and your retirement plans or future career goals. This portion tips over into Leg Three of the stool, but from a financial point of view that affects your wants and needs.

You will have to decide on what your minimum level of annual income needed to cover your expenses. You will also have to consider the timeframe of possible income loss and capital erosion if you are transitioning. You also have to calculate the optimal level of annual income needed to maintain a desired lifestyle. Do not forget to factor in extraordinary events such as the funding of weddings, children, education, holidays, vacation, medical and even nursing home considerations.

So your team will analyze all of this information and will work with you to create an action plan that will be fully developed for implementation. Again, as in Leg One this action plan will include what has to be done, the timetable for it and who is going to be responsible for accomplishing that particular item. So that is the activity that will be required in Leg Two of the stool.

The advisors who have their respective processes complete most of the work on this leg of the stool - your success is dependent on the caliber of your wealth manager and estate attorney and so forth along with your goals and objectives. So it is a customized plan for you or your family. The main thing is to go through what some consider a painful process. But it's extremely important to get these questions asked and answered to develop the much needed (or necessary) action plan.

This is an area where the quarterback of the team will be assisting the business owner in several ways. This person normally would not be in directly involved in providing any of the activity here. They will be coordinating; the quarterback will be doing the follow up to make sure that each advisor is performing their important part of the process. This process is completed through a coordinated effort, a time where collaboration is of the utmost importance to the wealth managers, estate planning, tax planning, and other experts on your team.

The success of an individual's plan depends on who the business owner will be using as their advisors. It will be based on the advisor's background experience; their willingness to work with business owners and their ability to keep the business owner's plan as a priority. As I said earlier, most advisors are not used to working as a team in a process like this. This is evolutionary. Usually they are working in their world, in their silo with the clients, and they are not integrating the full Master Plan and taking that into consideration.

In Chicago, it is estimated there are approximately 30,000 financial advisors and wealth managers. Just in Chicago alone! So there are plenty of companies and organizations that provide these services, but like in any other profession very few good ones.

The most optimal person acting as your Quarterback would be a **Certified Exit Planning Advisor** (CEPA). During Leg Two, your quarterback will formulate a general assessment of your financial, estate and tax future. For instance, you would talk about possible and probable transfer methods and then formulate a draft of your plan. Then, if you do not have advisors, your Certified Exit Planning Advisor knows wealth managers, financial advisors, estate planners and tax planners that would have experience and capabilities in this area.

Now that you have a better understanding of the importance of the quarterback, their skills and how well they can integrate with the rest of your team, it's time to talk about the most-often disregarded element of the Master Plan: your personal plan.

The Master Plan

If you are unsure whether your current advisors can handle this type of transactions OR if you do not have an advisor in a particular area visit www.MasterPlanningInstitute.com
or text MPI to 58885
to gain resources that will help you through this process.

Dave and the Dysfunctional Family

The next story I want to share with you is about Dave. Dave runs a very successful family owned business but despite that, the company doesn't have a succession plan, and Dave is in his 80s.

Dave's son Mark left the company about four years prior, but when he proposed selling the company, he was able to negotiate all the terms that Dave wanted, as well as his control of the company for three years.

The entire family was really excited about the buyer, a private equity group that was well known and respected and Mark was really excited about how this group grew companies, often injecting new life into older businesses that could use some rejuvenation.

But Dave couldn't pull the trigger, and the buyer walked away.

Imagine being the son or daughter of someone who in the process of selling their company, made the deal falter on the table six or seven times. Mark believes that his dad couldn't make the transition because he was afraid of becoming irrelevant.

Dave's concept of self was wrapped up in his position as the

60

owner and founder of this company. He might have been able to keep a consultant position with the new owners, but even that had an expiration date to it.

"At his age," Mark explained about his father, "He just didn't want to lose everything that he had worked so hard for and that included the recognition and status."

Dave's decision, not to sell the business and give up control of the helm damaged his relationship with his family.

"He plans on dying in his successful business," Mark says. "To this day he claims that he wants to have a relationship with his family, but he feels like he can't because of his position with the company. He refuses to reach out to any of us; it's a very sad situation."

Dave wasn't trying to hurt his family by refusing to sell his business, he just does not have the skill set needed to walk away. A person in Dave's position will often think that he is making every right decision simply because there is no evidence to the contrary – at least from his point of view.

How a Master Plan would have been beneficial in this situation is that it would have highlighted, in an objective way, all evidence that points to what is the right thing for everyone involved. It takes the "personal" out of the situation, but it also helps the owner make plans and keep their momentum past the sale of the business.

Over the years, the family brought in business coaches and family counselors and Mark, himself, used every tool that he could find to bring a resolution to the situation that suited everyone before he had to walk away.

It's hard for some people to deal with their mortality and that's tied so closely to dealing with the loss or sale of a business, as that's many entrepreneur's life. It can make a family member seem stingy or greedy.

"People fall in love with their bank accounts. I think my father treats every dollar like it could just disappear like it was his life that he was protecting," Mark says about his father. "But he's not just his dollars. Considering his resources and his intelligence, he could do so much more with his resources."

CHAPTER SIX

Develop Your Life Plan (The Most Neglected Leg)

They say that when people retire that they go through five of the seven stages of grief. It's not that they feel their lives are over, it's just that they've managed to live so long on the day to day highs and lows of their business. And, when you spend so much time invested in one venture, it can seem like there is nothing else left for you when you're done. That's why it's time to discuss probably the most neglected, forgotten, and most important leg of the stool...your life plan.

Most business owners are so busy working in their business that they have never taken the time to step away or stand back and take a look at their life while enjoying what they are doing. Have you given time to think about what happiness looks like in the future, post-exit strategy? What is your personal situation like in your business? You have not had to plan for some of the simplest everyday items or worry about a resume or anything else like that about your future.

I'm sure this is not the first time you've heard someone talk about this, but this might be the first time you've been 'challenged' to think about YOUR life. I've seen this too many times to count; your personal plans are lacking in comparison to your business plans - primarily due to your absorption with your business. If you are honest, more than likely someone close to you, like a spouse or child has attempted to get you interested in something outside of your work!

In Leg Three, we drill down and determine are you doing the things you want to be doing. Are you accomplishing the things you want to be achieving? Is your business what you want to be doing or do you want to do something different? Are there any goals or objectives that you are not fulfilling?

We take a deep look to answer these questions and come up again with an action plan that will determine a lifestyle life plan that will be the blueprint for your future and your legacy. We will consider items such as do you want to work in the business for two or three years after you exit the business? Do you just want to work in the business and plan for a transfer much later in your life? Or do you require a contingency plan in case something should happen to you health-wise or that proverbial truck hits you?

Some other considerations include considering whether or not you will have discussions on how to handle your desired level of confidentiality (in case you decide to transfer your business) and plan the appropriate strategy for handling your confidentiality concerns. This will include discussion on how to discuss the business with your family, with personal advisors and key employees.

From these discussions, which are purely personal, we will then develop your plan for the third act of your life. If you have a family to consider, you'll find that this phase of the process is one of the most important.

The Quarterback's role during this phase is to have those

The Master Plan

tough conversations with you (and the family) about your activity and attitude towards your home life, work life, hobbies, and philanthropy. The Quarterback will also want to discuss your vision of what kind of legacy you want to leave.

Another topic we explore is what is going to provide you with a happy life. The result of the activity in Leg Three is an action plan. This action plan will provide ideas and opportunities   for you to explore, so you can plan and act accordingly.

At the beginning of this chapter, I mentioned that this was often the most neglected part of the process. Too often, business owners are so driven to create financial security for their family and those within the company that there isn't time to think about how their lives would be without the business. As an entrepreneur, you are wired to think continually about the health and growth of your business, something that doesn't align with making plans for your life post-business.

Once we begin to dig a little deeper, it's not uncommon to unearth topics that go beyond the capabilities and strengths of the quarterback. When this situation occurs, the quarterback will bring in **business psychologists** or family planning experts who have specific experience in dealing with these matters.

This is a very important part of the process since this not only impacts you, the owner of the business, but your family, employees, clients and others working in and around the business. For the Master Plan to be successful, it has got to be well thought out, keeping all aspects in mind.

When a business owner neglects this step, it is almost like someone comes and turns the switch off on the owner. In the book Smartcuts, the author quotes Susan Bradley as saying, "Momentum has been building for a while…and then there's this feeling of this drop into an abyss. It's like the beams of a house have gone away, and you have to build from the inside out. That sense is paralyzing. It affects our cognitive functioning."*

There have been studies that follow the ultra-successful and the ultra-rich after they reach the top – many are profoundly depressed. It's not because they left their business, but it's because they have lost the sense of inertia that has given them the 'beams in their house' for so long. Proper planning before the exit will diminish the negative emotional aspects that come with exiting your business.

The Master Plan

This step is not only FOR YOU, but also everyone that will be impacted by your transition out of the company. Having these conversations, regarding how you might react to certain situations, or how other people will react to you after you transfer out of your business, is critical.

Sometimes when I meet with clients and we talk about this step, they seem to have it all figured out and yet they have never taken the time to discuss it with those closest to them.

Let me explain.

After exiting his company, Thomas built a 2500 sq.ft. building where he could work on his hobbies, have space away from family and friends, and maintain a quiet, secluded place to read the Wall Street Journal. This was not a well thought out plan, and Thomas should have had discussions with his spouse regarding their plans as a couple and not just the owner's desires.

I also mentioned working with a family business that had established only two of the three legs of the stool – the story of Mark and his father, David. Right before the sale, Dave's seller's remorse overcame him. At the last minute, he could not go through with the sale because he did not take the time to follow the exercise on how his life would be when he awoke each morning and didn't have to drive to the office. Understandably so, as this was something he had been doing for the last 20, 30 years without much personal identification or time away from his 'mistress', the business.

This didn't just cause his suffering; it affected his entire family. He has three children that, despite having worked in the business prior to the Exit, are now not involved in this business at all and some have severed family relationships due to the stress that went along with the situation.

I realize this portion of the Master Plan might be the most painful for some to go through and yet, for others, it's liberating! Be assured that no matter which category you fall under, the more time you spend planning for this BEFORE the actual event, the better your life will be after that special day of liquidity - for you and those you love!

So, now that you have a better understanding as to not just why this part of the stool is so important but how it impacts so many different lives, the next chapter will provide a seat to place these three legs under!

How prepared are you with this portion of the process?
Whether you have given this little, much or no thought at all, we encourage you to take intentional steps in this part of the process. To help you begin thinking through how you will structure your time, how you will react to the way people will react to you, what will your role will be in life and many other important questions that deserve your time and thoughts, visit www.MasterPlanningInstitute.com
or text MPI to 58885
to take two very informative questionnaire's that will pave a clear path!

> "If you don't design your own life plan, chances are you'll fall into someone else's plan. And guess what they have planned for you? Not much."
> Jim Rohn

The Trucking Company

When Melissa and her husband decided to sell their trucking company, they wanted to be extra cautious.

"We didn't want to disturb our customers or our employees. We had to figure out if we could sell the business without destroying or disrupting it," Melissa told me.

They had five children who were all sick and tired of the trucking industry. One of their children was being groomed to take over, but when she sat down with her parents and she told them that after receiving her business degree and working at the company for three years, she was only sticking around because of her parents.

That was the last tie that was holding the couple to the business, and they decided to sell. Because of their wishes, it was important that any offers they receive not only be right in terms of the financial compensation, but it also had to be 'right' in terms of the owners wishes: keeping the company operating at its current location.

There was an emotional component that had to be taken care of, there were people who the couple had become close to, that would be staying behind with the company. They had spent years building a reputation as a great place to work and building a community of their employees. When it came time to sell, they wanted to make sure the company remained an active part of the community and that the employees wouldn't have to relocate to keep their jobs.

That's part of what made their sale so successful. The company had spent thirty years building the brand and the good faith of the company, and the new owners were willing to pay for it.

"Our first step was building our team. We needed advisors, attorneys, accountants, business people... we needed help because we were committed to making the transition as smooth as possible, and we weren't sure how to do it on our own," Melissa adds.

Melissa and her husband were confident in their plans because they knew they had the right team in place to make it work, giving them a peace of mind and the Master Plan to hold it all together.

CHAPTER SEVEN

Ta-Dah' The Master Plan

When we talk about the seat of the stool, we're talking about the portion of the strategy that represents the transfer methods available to businesses. Once we have developed the three legs of the stool, the business owner is now deriving all the benefits of the Master Plan.

Now that we have all three legs of the stool fully developed, its time to discuss the options. Because one of the best benefits of spending time in creating a complete Master Plan Exit Strategy is that you now have options you more than likely would not have had if not going through the 2-5 year preparation period!

For example, do you want to continue in the business as the owner? Now that the business is functioning at its peak, and the business is organized and systems have been built for dynamic performance, this option might be the best one for you. But it's just one option available to you. You wouldn't make a business decision without the full picture, so you can't make decisions about exiting your business without knowing all of the various options and their impact on your plan, your family and your personal needs.

There are a total of seven options that are available to you once you are ready to exit being a business owner.

Remember, it takes two to five years to fully develop and act upon the Master Plan Exit Strategy process (all aspects of the stool) for it to be effective. When you arrive at your 'exit goal' you are now in a position to receive all of the benefits of having completed the Master Plan. These include, but are not limited to, focusing on a value creation management style. You are achieving greater cash flow; you have prepared yourself and the business for unplanned emergency situations. You have a plan for preserving your lifestyle, and you continue to be in control of your business and your life. This provides the basis for company continuity, family stability, management stability and many more benefits that provide satisfaction to your life's existence.

So this chapter is dedicated to where you go from here.

The good news is there are plenty of options; you make the decision of which would be the best for you and your family.

7 Potential Ways to Transfer Your Business

(As provided by Rob Slee, noted author, entrepreneur, and investment banker - Please, Google and look him up!)

1. *Selling the business to your Employees.* This can be done through Employee Stock Option Plans (ESOPS), management buyouts and insurance.
2. *Transferring the Business To Family.* That could be done through outright gifts, annuities, grats, etc.
3. *Transfer the business to a charitable trust.* Charitable remainder trusts and charitable lead trusts necessitate

additional legal work, something most professional estate planning attorneys can assist with.

4. *Transfer to Co-Owners*. Those methods are buy/sell agreements, Dutch options, Russian Roulette.
5. *Sell Your Business and Retire*. One and Two-Step private sales or auction sales.
6. *Sell and Continue*. This method would be consolidation play, recapitalizations, buy and build, and roll ups.
7. *Go Public*. This includes going with initial public offerings and direct public offerings and reverse mergers - very few privately held business would use this channel.

Each channel and transfer method has different company valuations. That is why completing Leg Two of the stool can help the owner determine which transfer channel meets their goals and objectives.

A lot of business owners will select the sale transfer channel of selling and continuing. This method provides them with an opportunity to get a bite of the apple now by selling a percentage of the business and getting a competent partner, usually a private equity group and then five to ten years later getting an opportunity for the second bite of the apple when the company is sold by the owner and their partners. This is an ideal transfer method for companies with growth potential to partner with groups who have experience in growing companies and exiting them after an appropriate amount of time. This is a great opportunity for younger business owners.

The sale and retire method is exactly how it sounds, the owner wants to get out of their business and retire from that particular activity and this transfer channel has been planned for in the Leg Two and Leg Three analysis.

Comments about both sale transfer methods – depending on the size of the company, the owner and the team quarterback should select an investment banker or business broker who has had success in their particular industry or experience in using these two alternatives. The process of choosing a banker or broker will include, but is not limited to, understanding all the activities that have been developed and acted upon in the process of the legs of the stool. They will then research the potential buyer population that may be interested in the owners' business opportunities and will provide those for the owner's approval. Other tools are a confidential business profile (a one-page sanitized version of the business normally referred to as a 'teaser') to qualify buyer prospects.

Confidentiality agreements will be executed by the buyer prospects and business owners. After receiving confidentiality agreements from the prospects, the prospects will be furnished with a confidential business review, which will have a complete description of the company and its strengths and weaknesses as developed from Leg One of the stool. The confidential business review is a selling document and will provide the road map for the continuation of the process or journey.

After the buyer prospect has analyzed the confidential business review, they will submit a letter of interest indicating their value range and major conditions to closing. The owner's team will then select the prospects they want to invite in for visits from these letters of interest. These buyer prospect visits should be well coordinated by the banker or broker.

All of these steps are important. A good banker and/or broker will be utilizing proper procedures to maintain confidentiality throughout this entire process including recommending casual dress for the buyer prospect visits if that is the Company's dress

The Master Plan

code. After each visit, the buyer prospect who is interested in moving forward will be asked to submit a letter of intent by a certain, specified date. So the auction process that is being used will provide multiple looks and multiple offers for the business owner to choose from. The business owner and their team will then get together, pick the buyer prospect they want to 'go to the dance with' and develop a finalized letter of intent and put the other buyer prospects on hold.

So now the owner has a letter of intent from a buyer prospect that they want to do business with and a backup (in case something should fall through with the primary prospect). Once a final letter of intent has been developed and executed, the letter of intent provides the roadmap for closing. This is commonly known as the red zone of selling a business. It is imperative that action steps be developed, timetables presented, parties responsible for these action steps listed, and followed up diligently by the banker or broker to completion.

The remaining activities include buyer due diligence, buyers-sellers due diligence and buyer-seller documentation (personal sale contracts) which should be a 60 – 90-day process depending on the situation. Once the buyer and the owner are in the 'red zone' things must be performed diligently and on time. The rhythm and chemistry of any transaction depend on the execution of that timing.

The work that the owner has performed in the Master Planning process and the results of the auction sales process will produce maximum value for the business owner to achieve their goals and objectives. For instance, the analysis and activity performed on the second leg of the stool on a 20 million dollar transaction could result in savings of millions of dollars just from the effort of tax planning.

Now that we've walked through the different options you'll have a 30,000 foot view, we move onto some of the frequently asked questions as I am speaking to groups of business owners and their advisors in the next chapter.

If you are interested in accessing Pete's Top Trusted Organizations be sure to visit
www.MasterPlanningInstitute.com or text MPI to 58885

Frequently Asked Questions

My hope that you now have a better feel of:
Why it's important to begin planning now for the day that is inevitable ... the day you exit your business as an owner;
the next steps for you and your organization.

Now that you have seen the process from a 30,000 foot view, the main strategies you'll need to have in place, all four components, the three legs of the stool and the seat, and that to do it alone would take you out of managing your business... I want to share with you the questions that many people have once they have heard me present this concept!

Q. What are some of the personal thoughts or conversations I should have before starting the Master Planning process?
A. You have to determine whether you have the discipline and capabilities to structure the time for the process. In my opinion, you cannot run your business and do this process. You will need good advisors, but it will be well worth it. In Leg Three, considerations would be about how people would react to you exiting. If your personal identity is tied up in your company; what would you do if you exited? Stuff like that would be in the process of the question and answer steps.

Q. I am involved in a family owned business, why should I look at proceeding with a Master Plan?
A. The answer would be 'it is a very risky situation with family businesses, only 30% survive to the second generation, 12% to the third generation and 3% to the fourth generation

and beyond. You do not want to be part of these statistics.

Q. Why should I begin Leg One of the stool and have a company valuation?

A. Merger and acquisition experts believe that business owner's unrealistic expectations of company value are the biggest obstacle to exit, sale or boost transfers.

Q. Why is it important to have a value creation management style versus a lifestyle management process?

A. When business owners begin to view their businesses as investments and not jobs, they begin making much better financial decisions. Many owners do not appreciate the amount of risk that truly exists in their business. Buyers or successors to your company will pay you a multiple of your company's cash flow depending on the risk they perceive in your business. The higher the perceived risk, the lower the price someone will pay. Understanding your true risk in your business is a large part of the Master Planning process.

Q. Why is it so important to know my exit options?

A. Too many owners of privately held businesses believe that selling is their only way to exit. They do not understand their options for exiting their business or the various valuation techniques involved in these options. As a result many of them seek the advice of transactional advisors and engage their services with much less than perfect information.

Q. What advice do you give to people that are starting businesses?

A. That is easy. I believe business owners who are starting

78

their business should start a business with the end in mind. Start from day one on focusing and using the Master Planning process. That will guarantee their success at the end of their business tenure.

Q. What do buyers think of the master planning process?

A. Private equity groups and strategic buyer recognize the value of a well-defined Master Plan. These sophisticated investors will not invest in a business without a detailed Master Plan. Thus, every business owner should do the same whether you are starting out or whether you are a few years away from planned transitions. These buyers understand the value of having a business owner know the strengths and weaknesses of their company, and the valuation of their company. The fact that they planned to retain most of the sale or exit proceeds because of completing Leg Two of the stool. Knowing they have a life plan about what they are going to be doing after they transition from their business is a very sophisticated and impressive factor with buyers.

Q. Isn't going through a Master Plan costly?

A. There is no doubt that a business owner going through Master Planning will have to invest in the Master Planning process. Depending on the size of the business, they could invest anywhere from $50,000 to $500,000 or more. But with a good Master Plan they should derive value that will be equal to or at least an increase in their exit multiple from normal to as high an increase of one-times multiple to two-times multiple. So to me the real question is, isn't it costly NOT going through a Master Plan Process?

Q. What is wrong with just having a lifestyle business and why should we be concerned about value creation?

A.   Many businesses are what we call lifestyle businesses. They are businesses that meet the needs and wants of the owners and their family. Often, their lifestyles are expanded to the level of income created by the business. These same owners are doing very little to save for or plan for the future. They also think that everything is going to work out for the business to meet their retirement needs and that they will be able to sell their business when they are ready for the price they want. They do not realize that they are not creating value beyond the risk of their cost of capital discussed earlier in the book.

Q. Why do I need to write plans if I have all these plans and ideas thoroughly cemented in my mind?

A. Studies show people who put plans down in writing are 70% more likely to accomplish them than people who do not.

Q. Why do I need all these advisors to assist me in my Master Plan?

A. Master planning is an integrated approach using all the skills of professionals necessary to help a business owner develop and implement a successful transition plan and Master Plan.   It is very difficult to receive these types of value services through any one particular organization.

Q. What is so important about the timing of my master plan?

A. Because all of us are human, as brought out earlier in the book, we do not know what is going to happen to us tomorrow, next week, next month or next year. That is why it is important

The Master Plan

to develop a Master Plan and be in the process of implementing a Master Plan to safeguard us against the risk of being human. And also fulfilling our responsibilities that we have to ourselves, our family, our employees who depend on us, our customers and suppliers is so important and responsible.

CHAPTER EIGHT

Conclusion

The completion of a Master Plan functions as an insurance policy for business owners by eliminating various business risks.

It insures the basic goals and objectives of exit planning, those being:

1.   Maximizing the value of the business,

2.   Getting planned personally from an estate, tax and financial point of view so that when transition, transfer events take place owners are able to keep a much larger percentage of what they receive, and

3.   The deliverance of a life plan that will provide balance and fulfillment for the business owner today and in the future.

I want to see everyone become successful and obtain their life-long goals and objectives. This book is written expressly for that cause and no other. Business owners are human, and because they are, they have to take action now to act on their responsibilities to themselves, their family, their employees who depend on them, their customers and vendors. Now is the time to ACT! What ever I can do to help...ask now! I am here to help you to help yourself in achieving those life long goals and objectives!

If you haven't already visited
www.MasterPlanningInstitute.com or text MPI to 58885
to access the resources throughout this book, you'll want to!
By registering your copy of this book you'll have access to my
team of attorneys, estate planners and other advisors through
future videos and podcasts

About the Author

Peter G. Christman is an experienced entrepreneur, corporate executive, coach, mentor, and investment banker. After spending 25 years as an investment banker with other firms, Peter Christman founded The CHRISTMAN Group, LLC to provide middle market business owners with a comprehensive and integrated suite of services that simplify the exit planning process while maximizing the value of the client's business. The Christman Group mantra is that we want our clients to be "SET" for life.

During his 30+year career Pete has successfully sold more than 200 companies in a wide variety of industries. Transactions have ranged in size from several million dollars to over one hundred million dollars.

Peter was the co-founder of the Chicago office of a national middle market M&A firm where he continually earned that firm's "Top Gun" award, which recognizes the firm's most successful dealmakers.

Peter is also the co-founder of the Exit Planning Institute, which educates and certifies business advisors on how to implement business owner "exit planning" into their practices. The Institute has developed its own proprietary certification program.

Peter is an entertaining and sought after public speaker who has given hundreds of presentations and seminars on the benefits of exit planning and the middle market mergers and acquisition process. He has also written articles on the importance of the exit planning process. He is the Co-Author of the book, "The Ten Trillion Opportunity".

The Master Plan

Before becoming a middle market investment banker, Pete spent 17 years in high-level marketing and management positions with both Ford Motor Company and Xerox Corporation. Pete is an active member of industry organizations such as ACG, AMAA, MBBI, TEI, TVC, and has served on many Boards of organizations and companies.

Endnotes

Exit Planning Institute 2013 Business Owner Survey | www.exit-planning-institute.org

Pfingsten Partners LLC. | www.PfingstenPartners.com

Smartcuts: How Hackers, Innovators and Icons Accelerate Success by Shane Snow

Made in the USA
Las Vegas, NV
15 July 2024

92353934R00049